HOW TO WRITE A POSTAL CARD.

(An excerpt from James Nichols' 1886 book, *Safe Methods of Business*.)

1. A card should be dated either on the upper right-hand corner, or on the lower left-hand corner.

2. The writer's full name should be signed to it.

3. If an answer is required, the writer's full post-office address should be given, or underscored by the person to whom

4. In writing to a postal card, as it is not proper for its return, it its destination. Notes of invitation, etc., which society prescribes certain polite forms be observed.

5. Never write a demand or request for money on a postal card. It is disrespectful to the person receiving it.

6. Postal cards can be sent to Canada and Mexico.

Post Card

CORRESPONDENCE

ADDRESS O

*Grand sights,
Glorious times —
Wish you were here.*

Enthusia Small

*Greeting from
Naperville*

Postmark Naperville

An A to Z History

by Marcia Koffron Mackenbrock
and Sharon Ridgeway Weber

Published by Enthusia Small
http://www.postmarknaperville.com

Graphic Design by Lisa D. Klingbeil
West Branch Studio, Naperville, IL
design@westbranchstudio.com

Printing and binding by Worzalla
Stevens Point, WI

This book is dedicated to Naper School
where kindred spirits first met,
and to McTavish the Scottie,
our muse and our comic relief.

Naper School 1928 -

Acknowledgments

To all those who helped us via phone and email, through interviews and meetings, by proofreading and just plain listening, we thank you for your support, your encouragement and your gift of time.

City of Naperville: Mayor A. George Pradel, Gary Karafiat
Positively Naperville: Stephanie Penick
Naperville Heritage Society: Louise Howard, Sue Degges
Naperville Sun: Laurie K. Kagann
Naperville Century Walk: Brand Bobosky
YMCA: Dave Bast, Jane Bowers, Barbara Johnson
North Central College: Kimberly Jacobson Butler, Jean Morrison, Cody Smith, John Rygiewicz
Naperville Municipal Band: Ron Keller
Anderson's Bookshops: Becky Anderson Wilkins
Minuteman Press: Ray Kinney
Nichols Library: Marcia Lebeau, Sue Prindiville, Betty Wampach
Naperville Park District: Sameera Luthman
Lake County Discovery Museum: Kathryn Hamilton-Smith
United States Postal Service, Washington, D.C.: Angela Smith
Don Clark Stamps, Aurora, IL

And also to: Frank Alston, Mary Ann Bobosky, the Michael Burd Family, Rachel Conklin, Katie Cook, Paul Dahlquist, Mary Garry, Casey Klingbeil, Lynette Klingbeil, Jean Lacher, Joyce and Wayne Lipski, Fred Mackenbrock, the Naper School archives, Bonnie Olson, George and Adele Ridgeway, Tim and Tom Shiou, Mary Tendick, and Milan Weber.

ISBN 0-9754040-0-8

ENTHUSIA SMALL

[En-thu-si-asm All]

Dear Reader,

Naperville, Illinois - What a place! Its history stretches back to 1831 and what a lively history it has been!

Join us on a post card journey through the years and around the town. Every page tells the tale of a past that will surprise, inform and delight you.

MKM & SRW

Caution!

K = N but N = Y

A = R but R = F

B = S but S = J

Q = E but E = D

This is not your ordinary alphabet book. The letters move from A to Z but the subjects shift before your eyes. Better not blink or you'll lose the flow.

Open the cover and enter the world of early Naperville. From All Aboard to Zany, every page boasts vintage post cards, historic stamps, photos past and present and text that ties it all together. Combined, they are an album of the dynamic community Napervillians proudly call home.

All post cards are authentic to the era of historic Naperville. The stamps span over 100 years and are thumbnail sketches of each subject. Quiz yourself on questions throughout the book before checking in back to find the answers. Follow the page borders for additional fascinating facts. And whatever you do, don't miss the picture post card messages. There's more to those names than meets the eye for they, too, are a part of the story.

Most of all, have fun on your trip through time. It's a journey that is guaranteed to make you say, "I didn't know that!"

T = M but M = I

W = P but P = O

V = G and L but G = H and L = P

Table of Contents

A All Aboard = Railroad

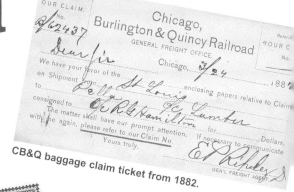

CB&Q baggage claim ticket from 1882.

Naperville did not always have a train running through town. As a matter of fact, there was a time when Naperville refused to allow train tracks anywhere near it. Townsfolk wanted no part of those noisy steam engines and blaring whistles. After all, they had Old Plank Road. Big mistake. Almost overnight Naperville went from Illinois boom town to Illinois ghost town. Everyone headed north to the train in Wheaton.

It did not take long for people to realize that if they were to prosper, they needed the train to take their goods to markets throughout the country. In 1864 the Chicago, Burlington and Quincy added Naperville to its route and the little town was on the grow again. The railroad found Naperville to be such a scenic stop that it created Burlington Park, where the railroad crossed the DuPage River. It brought city folk from Chicago, as many as 10,000 on a sunny weekend, to enjoy a day in the country.

There was a boat house with boats, a dining and dance pavilion, a bowling alley, a shooting gallery and a merry-go-round that was brought all the way from California, most likely by train. Rides cost five cents each.

Sadly, Burlington Park was closed in 1899 and the 60-acre park was sold to the DuPage Forest Preserve in 1922 for $82.50. What a fun place it must have been.

CB&Q stock certificate dated 1880.

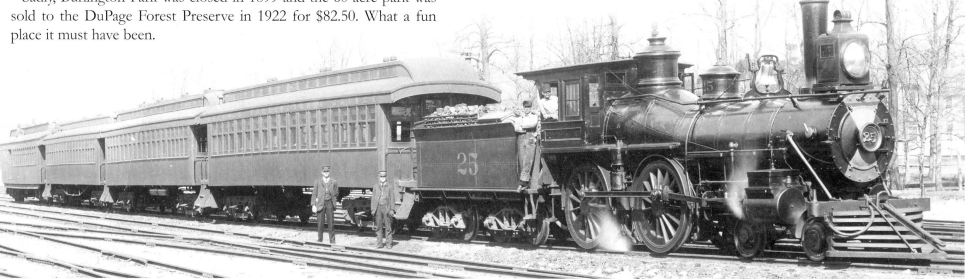

0m
Chicago

13m
Riverside

18m
Hinsdale

22m
Downers Grove

29m
Naperville

R R

CHICAGO BURLINGTON & QUINCY R.R.

3c UNITED STATES POSTAGE — THE BALTIMORE & OHIO RAILROAD CHARTERED FEB. 28, 1827 — 125 YEARS OF RAIL TRANSPORTATION

Scenes from Burlington Park circa 1880.

Locomotive 1870s USA 2c

POST CARD

PLACE POSTAGE STAMP HERE

THE ADDRESS... ON T...

...SIDE FOR CORRESPONDENCE.

...aught train to Naperville. Ready for a day away from the city. Traveled 29 miles in 95 minutes. Full speed ahead, Spike Hammer

"The Old Railroad Depot" by Lester Schrader. Courtesy Naperville Heritage Society "Brushstrokes of the Past" history gallery.

NAPERVILLE 28

Trains Leave.						May 23, 1869.		Trains Arrive.			
Pass	Pass	Pass	Exps	Pass	Mls	STATIONS.	Mls	Pass	Exps	Pass	Pass	Pass
P. M.	P. M.	P. M.	P M.	A. M.				P. M.	P. M.	P. M.	A. M.	A. M.
†4 30	†5 45	†3 00	11 30	†7 45	0	....Chicago 1....	263	†8 15	†6 45	†4 30	†8 15	†9 40
5 13	6 28	3 48	12 20	8 25	13	....Riverside......	250	7 3	6 02	3 48	7 25	9 00
5 2	6 50	4 04	12 39	8 45	18	....Hinsdale......	245	7 1	5 47	3 33	7 07	8 45
5 40	7 05	4 14	12 52	8 58	22	...Downer's Grove...	241	7 05	---	3 22	6 55	8 35
6 00	7 24	4 32	J 15	9 18	29	....Naperville....	234	6 50	5 15	3 02	6 35	8 15
6 3	7 45	5 00	1 50	9 50	3	....Aurora.....	225	6 3	4 52	2 40	6 15	7 55
6 3					3	....West Aurora..	2 4	P. M.			A. M.	7 52
6 4		5 13	2 08	10 04	43	.....Oswego......	220	6 1	---	2 25		7 43

Train schedule from 1869. Note the Naperville stop.

QUESTION: If 10,000 people paid five cents each to ride the merry-go-round, how much money would be made?

B Batter Up = Softball

POST CARD

Correspondence   Address Only

Picnicked on 2nd base
in Kendall Park. Could
almost hear the roar of
the crowd.

From the bleachers,
Homer Fielder

Guaranteed Real Photo and British Manufacture

1869-1969
UNITED STATES 6c
PROFESSIONAL BASEBALL

What do you do when times are tough? Play Ball! And Naperville was a baseball sweet spot. During the Great Depression years of the 1930s, when jobs and money were scarce, the game of eleven-inch, underhand, fast-pitch softball took the country by storm. Teams popped up all over with names like the Roseland Merchants, the Joliet Rivals and the Bismark Brewers. These were not professional players, but industrial workers who practiced and played on evenings and weekends.

Not to be struck out, Naperville had its own teams, one of which was the Kroehler Aristocrats, made up of men from the Kroehler Manufacturing Company. The Kroehler Company built a lighted softball field with aboveground dugouts and a concession stand. A sound truck blared the play-by-play for the entire town to hear. Green was the Kroehler color, so uniforms were green with gold trim and letters. For travel to away games players piled into the back of a Kroehler furniture van and took to the road hoping for a clean sweep of their rivals.

The glory days of industrial softball ended on December 7, 1941, when many players stepped up to the plate to defend their country after the attack on Pearl Harbor, when the United States entered World War II.

DEC 24 9 AM 1910 NAPERVILLE ILL

Kroehler Aristocrats softball team, 1919. Courtesy Naperville Heritage Society.

KROEHLER MFG. CO

1830 1939 3 CENTS UNITED STATES POSTA

33 USA

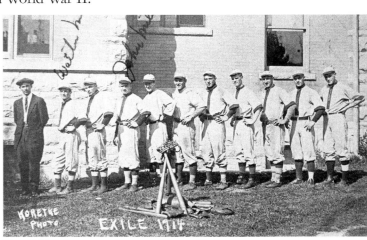

KORETKE PHOTO   EXILE 1914

"Pillars of the Community" mural, Chicago Avenue and Main Street. Courtesy Naperville Century Walk.

The 1914 Exiles team. Courtesy Naperville Sun.

QUESTION: In 1963 Naperville won the Illinois State Little League Championship. What was the name of the winning team?

C Check It Out = Library

It's hard to imagine Naperville, the city that reads, without a library, but that was the case for the first sixty-seven years the town existed. Then along came a North Central College professor and book publisher named James L. Nichols, who realized the importance of books for everyone. Upon his death, he left $10,000 in his will for the town to build a library.

The first Nichols Library was built on Washington Street in 1898. Opening day was set for September 22, but there was one small problem. NO BOOKS!

That's right. All the money was needed to construct the building. Nothing was left for books. But that did not stop the good folks of Naperville. Approximately 300 people attended the grand opening and almost all brought a book to donate. That's how the library started and that's community spirit.

Miniature Room in Nichols Library lobby. Press the button to relight early library days.

Glow by Josef Albers USA 15c
Learning never ends

Yours very truly,
J. L. Nichols

America's
A B C
Libraries
X Y Z
USA 20c
Legacies To Mankind

N P L
Naperville Public Libraries
#1 PUBLIC LIBRARY
1999 NATIONAL RANK
100,000 + POPULATION

A Nation of
Readers
USA 20c

USA 4c
A PUBLIC THAT READS A ROOT OF DEMOCRACY

POST
MADE IN U.S.A.   FOR CORRESPONDENCE
Found it! First Nichols Library. Books long gone but I know just where to find 'em. Off to the new one.
Itching for a good read,
Booker Dailey
RIES 971 B

First Nichols Library at 110 S. Washington Street.

Nichols Library, Naperville, Ill.

One of James Nichols' popular business guides.

SAFE METHODS for BUSINESS

Longest serving librarian, Mary Barbara Egermann, affectionately known as Matie.

QUESTION: Approximately how many books does Nichols Library own today?

Corn Pone

Stoneground Cornbread

Shoo-fly Pie

Beater Biscuits

Lincoln Cake

Corn Dodgers

D Daily Bread = Grist Mill

Courtesy Naperville Sun.

grist (grist) n. to rub away, grind down; 1. grain that is to be or has been ground; esp. a batch of such grain. 2. [Colloq.], a quantity or lot.

RURAL AMERICA

U.S. 10¢

KANSAS HARD WINTER WHEAT 1874-1974

POST CARD
THIS SIDE FOR THE ADDRESS ONLY

Great monument in Pioneer Park. Site of the old grist mill. Have a whole new appreciation for my sandwich!

Leaving no crumbs,

Stoney Miller

1829 1929

"DU PAGE COUNTY PIONEER PARK"
DEDICATED WITH GRATEFUL REVERENCE
TO THE MEN AND WOMEN OF DU PAGE COUNTY

THIS TRACT IS PART OF THE ORIGINAL GRANT
TO THE FIRST WHITE SETTLER BAILEY HOBSON

THESE MILLSTONES ARE FROM THE HOBSON
MILL BUILT ON THE SOUTH IN 1834 ONE OF THE
FIRST IN THIS PART OF THE STATE

THE FOREST PRESERVE COMMISSION OF
DU PAGE COUNTY MADE POSSIBLE THIS PARK

DEDICATED JULY 4TH, 1929

1929 dedication plaque in Pioneer Park on Washington Street.

Original grist stones from Hobson Mill built in 1834.

Like some bread with your PB&J? Not so fast! If you were an early Naperville pioneer and wanted to enjoy a slice of bread, you had to grow the grain yourself, harvest it, find a mill to grind it into flour and bake it in your own oven. The growing, gathering and baking could be done at home, but the milling was another matter because early Naperville did not have its own grist mill. Wagons would have to be loaded with harvested grain and several days travel would be required to find a mill in another town fifty miles away. It didn't take long for the community to decide it needed its own mill and many of the settlers worked together to help get it built.

So busy was the new mill that horse-drawn wagons would line up and wait overnight to have their grain ground between the huge mill stones. Men would sleep in their wagons or across the river in the Bailey Hobson home while waiting their turn. The old grist mill may be gone but the original mill stones were saved and converted into a monument by the Daughters of the American Revolution. They stand today in Pioneer Park for all to see.

QUESTION: **Where do you think early settlers acquired mill stones of such immense size?**

Eat, Meet & Greet = Downtown

Close your eyes for a minute and take a step back in time. Imagine yourself in downtown Naperville in 1900 when the census listed the population as 2,600. Roads are unpaved and horses are everywhere. Sidewalks are made of boards built 2 ½ feet above the dirt roads to make it easier to step from a carriage onto the planks. Hitching posts line the streets to safely secure horses while people shop and greet each other.

Women might take a milk pail to the tin shop for repair or visit the cobbler to measure for a new pair of hand-made shoes. Men might stop at the blacksmith to have a horse reshod or a wagon repaired, then head for the Pre-Emption House to enjoy a cold drink and to catch up on news. Need to use a restroom or get a drink of water? You can find an outhouse and a hand pump behind the stores. As darkness comes, kerosene lamps are lit by the lamplighter as the good folks of Naperville wend their way home.

Raised boardwalks allowed shoppers level access from horse drawn buggies.

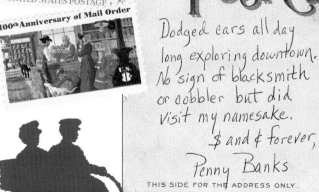

Dodged cars all day long exploring downtown. No sign of blacksmith or cobbler but did visit my namesake.
$ and ¢ forever,
Penny Banks

THIS SIDE FOR THE ADDRESS ONLY.

JEFFERSON AVE., NAPERVILLE, ILL.

Dirt streets were easy on horses but messy for people, so watch where you step!

QUESTION: Blast to the present. What is the population of Naperville today?

F First One In = Quarry

What Naperville hot spot is the coolest place to be in summer?   The answer is the quarry.

Did you ever wonder why Naperville has not one but three separate bodies of water along the Riverwalk? Long before you baited a fishhook or joined a swim team those deep, deep holes were filled with stone. From the early 1830s until 1904 huge slabs of Niagara limestone were cut and removed piece-by-piece by strong men and horse power. Quarrying was big business in Naperville. Landmark buildings such as the old Nichols Library, the Martin Mitchell Mansion and the Beach Bath House still stand on foundations made of local limestone. Tons more limestone was railroaded east to help Chicago rebuild after the Great Fire of 1871.

Dedication plaque, 1931, marking site of time capsule opened in 1981. Courtesy Naperville Sun.

This is our Beach. Bobby and I went down one day. NANCY

Beach scene, 1940, with original postcard message

The hot seat.

1933-1983 Civilian Conservation Corps USA 20c

Ready for a dip in 1952. Courtesy Naperville Sun.

Take your pick - Little Quarry (Netzley's Pond) for scenic beauty, Big Quarry for a dive and a dip or Paddleboat Lake for a smooth sail. All entertain thousands of patrons on any pleasant summer day. From opening day in 1932, when only three lifeguards kept nonstop watch for twelve straight hours, Centennial Beach has made a big splash with residents and guests. It is now one of the largest chlorinated pools in the world with sky-high safety standards.

Race you there!

QUESTION: How many gallons of water does Centennial Beach hold?

G Giddy-Up = Horses

"Horse Market Days" sculpture, Naper Settlement.
Courtesy Naperville Century Walk.

Stopped at livery stable and saw horse wearing a dress! Understand they call this a fly net. Pretty fancy fly flicker.

Buzz Ryder

Send more bug spray!

POST CARD

FOR CORRESPONDENCE

No flies on this mare. Check her out in the blacksmith shop at Naper Settlement, circa 1860.

Good Luck

The real horse market days drew quite a crowd to the Pre-Emption House. Courtesy Naperville Heritage Society.

Ever hear the expression, "one-horse town?" Whoa there! That certainly wasn't Naperville in its earliest days. No pioneer family could have conquered the hurdles of settling there without horses. Remember that there were no cars, trucks or trains; no trolleys, vans or planes. In those days you walked or you rode - on horseback. Horses plowed fields, pulled fire wagons, transported crops, hauled timber for Old Plank Road, delivered milk, marched in parades, raced on Sundays and helped quarry stone. And don't forget about the popular social event, Horse Market Days, where horses were bought, sold and traded. Name a job the pioneers faced and horses were sure to be involved.

On May 2, 1900 the first "horseless carriage" roared across town and the heyday of the horse began to fade. Automobiles gradually took over. Streets were paved, garages were built, mechanics were trained and those once hard-working horses were used more for the city's amusement than its survival. Now horsemanship in Naperville has come full circle. The rambunctious bronze steed outside Naper Settlement will be sure to catch your attention. And anyone hankering for a ride astride a real live four-legged mount can find recreational horseback riding within a stone's throw of where the original settlers stabled their steeds.

QUESTION: What unit of measure is used when discussing the height of horses?

Hip, Hip, Hooray = Celebrations

You are cordially invited . . . to a party! And Naperville is a town that loves a good party. Two of Naperville's best parties took place in the early 1900s. And they were **BIG**.

On Memorial Day weekend 1917, just a month after our country entered World War I, Naperville celebrated the progress and achievements made by the city since it was founded in 1831. The four-day extravaganza called the Naperville Home Coming Celebration included Old Citizens' Day, Patriotic Day, School and Church Day and Community Day. At six a.m. on day one, bells and whistles signaled the start of the festivities. Red, white and blue were the chosen colors. The Rose Maiden was the special song and the crimson scarlet geranium was the official flower.

The second big party, in 1931, was Naperville's Centennial Celebration to honor its first 100 years. A cast of hundreds performed a two-hour pageant of the town's history. Bands from Naper, Ellsworth and SS. Peter and Paul schools marched in a special Young Folks parade, and a descendant of John Naper was crowned Miss Naperville. On June 6, 1931, exactly 100 years to the day when Captain Joseph Naper first arrived, a special ceremony was held to unveil a memorial plaque renaming the old quarry Centennial Beach. Two years later Chicago held its World's Fair as the country slid into the Great Depression.

These celebrations were just the beginning for Naperville. Follow the border to party throughout the year.

Memorial Day Parade, 1917. Courtesy Naperville Sun.

Courtesy Naperville Heritage Society.

Early bicycle racers take their mark.
Courtesy Naperville Sun.

Centennial Day Parade, 1931.
Courtesy Naperville Sun.

THE SANDFORD MESSAGE

This town loves parades! Had a great spot to wave my flag as floats passed by.

Patriotically yours,

Joy Bunting

194 COPYRIGHT, SANDFORD CARD CO., DANSVILLE, N.Y.

POST CARD

WELCOME HOME   HOME COMING WEEK

YANKEE DOODLE

QUESTION: Naperville holds three parades annually. When are they?

I Incomparable = Park District

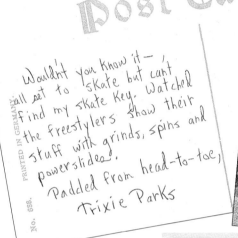

Post Card

Wouldn't you know it — all set to skate but can't find my skate key. Watched the freestylers show their stuff with grinds, spins and powerslides. Padded from head-to-toe,

Trixie Parks

PRINTED IN GERMANY.

No. 658.

Greetings from NAPERVILLE, ILL.

The National Arbor Day Foundation recognizes Naperville as an official Tree City USA.

Naperville
Park District™

SKATEBOARDING USA 33

Christmas USA 13c

WINTER PASTIME LITHOGRAPH BY N. CURRIER 1855

6c US

PLANT for more BEAUTIFUL PARKS

How does Naperville spell fun? P-A-R-K D-I-S-T-R-I-C-T! Established by referendum in 1966, it began offering programs for boys and girls in August of 1968. That first season opened with a bang - a boys' basketball program, ice rinks and ice skating races, an ice hockey league, two toboggan slides, a Christmas crafts program and a table tennis tournament.

Jump ahead to today and the choices have increased 100-fold. The park district now offers a mind-boggling 900 programs yearly. It also operates and maintains over 2,300 acres of land. This includes Centennial Beach, the Riverwalk and a large number of basketball, baseball, soccer and tennis facilities.

From its humble beginning the Naperville Park District has grown into its mission statement to be "a leader in providing leisure experiences that enhance the quality of life for our community." As a nationally recognized park district, it truly has something for everyone from infants to great-grandparents.

QUESTION: What does the word "incomparable" mean?

Just in Case = Fort Payne

Temporary Chicago refuge for women and children.

POST CARD

What a great old fort! Meet me at the lookout and we'll play pioneers. All fenced in, Hope Pickett

1833 U.S. POSTAGE 1933
CHICAGO CENTURY OF PROGRESS
FORT DEARBORN
1 CENT 1

Old Fort Dearborn in 1856, Chicago

REMOTE OUTPOST · NEW NATION BUILDING WESTWARD
USA 28¢

FORT PAYNE
NEAR THIS SITE IN 1832 A 100-FOOT SQUARE STOCKADE ENCLOSED BY WOODEN PICKETS, WITH TWO BLOCKHOUSES ON DIAGONAL CORNERS, WAS BUILT. HERE CAPTAIN MORGAN L. PAYNE AND HIS COMPANY OF FORTY-FIVE MEN PROTECTED THE SETTLERS FROM ROAMING SAUK INDIANS DURING THE BLACK HAWK WAR.
ERECTED BY
THE DUPAGE COUNTY HISTORICAL SOCIETY
AND
THE ILLINOIS STATE HISTORICAL SOCIETY, 1964

Naper Settlement's replica of Fort Payne, named for Capt. Paine. A curious spelling change.

What: Fort Payne, the only fort Naperville thought it needed.

When: 1832 as the Black Hawk War raged.

Where: At Fort Hill, just south of Chicago Avenue, on what is now the college campus of North Central. But that fort is long gone. A replica, built by volunteers in 1979, stands at Naper Settlement ready and waiting for your exploration.

Who: Soldiers and settlers alike rallied to the cause putting heads and hammers together to construct Fort Payne. Captain Morgan C. Paine led the crew; hence, his name guards the fort even today.

Why: With the threat of the unfriendly Sauk tribe coming too close to home for comfort, the area pioneer women and children were hustled off under cover of darkness by wagon train to the safety of Chicago's Fort Dearborn. After many weeks of almost unbearable living conditions, they returned intending to occupy the newly erected local fort - their safe haven until the coast was clear.

Why Not: Truth be told, it was the fort Naperville never needed! By the time it was ready, a treaty had been signed with Chief Black Hawk and peace was restored.

UNITED STATES POSTAGE
14 CENTS

MODEL OF THE FIRST FORT DEARBORN, BUILT IN 1803
CHICAGO HISTORICAL SOCIETY

QUESTION: Why were the settlers so anxious to leave the safety of Fort Dearborn?

K Kindred Spirits = North Central College

By all accounts North Central College deserves the setting and service of a place like Naperville. Or is it the other way around? It has been full-speed ahead for both the college and the city. The bonds forged long ago have held a solid, permanent and productive partnership that shows no signs of stopping.

Some would say that a sum of $25,000 - no small change in 1869 - was the best money Naperville ever spent. Many would say that you can't put a price on quality education. Thus when Plainfield's North-Western College sought a more accessible spot, Naperville welcomed it with open arms and open wallets. Competition for becoming the college site was keen; a college town could mean improvement of minds, morals and monetary success. NCC has accomplished all of that and more, and Naperville is ever grateful and the better for it.

Old Main Tower original bell, 1870, Old Main lobby.

OLD MAIN PLAZA

ABOVE: Mosaic of NCC seal, in floor of Old Main lobby.

Illinois Booster Day Parade, courtesy Mary Garry.

Postcard from NCC student, 1921.

CELINA-OHIO.
JULY 11, 19
DEAR FRIENDS:-
I ARRIVED
HOME O.K. AT 10.15 P.M.
FRIDAY. THE FOLKS ALL
KNEW ME. EVEN THE BABY
HE HAS CHANGED A LOT IN
A MONTH.
I CERTAINLY ENJOYED
THE SUMMER SCHOOL AND
MY ROOMING PLACE
HELPED CONSIDERABLY
TO KEEP ME FROM BECOMING
HOME-SICK.
SINCERELY,
M.O. HERMAN

Main Hall, North-Western College, Naperville, Ill.

Old Main was built of limestone quarried in Naperville.

Can you read the cornerstone inscription?

It says May 17, 1870.

QUESTION: What professional Chicago sports team played all of their 2001-2003 home games in the NCC stadium?

Look Who Won = Plow Matches

Site marker of first plowing match on former Alexander Brown farm.

Beating the clock behind a plow and ahead of everyone else was serious business in Naperville for 100 years beginning in 1877. A highlight on nearly everyone's entertainment calendar, Plow Match Days' reputation for competition, wholesome activities and plentiful food eventually drew farm families from all across the U.S. Anyone from anywhere could enter the races. In 1921 attendance topped 18,000. So eagerly anticipated were the Matches that it took very special circumstances like the World Wars to halt the event.

4-H booths, parades, ball games, auctions, farm progress displays, domestic arts tents - you'd find it all at Match Days. And all eyes were not on the ground; the 1920s brought airplane rides for visitors and in 1949 adventurous Match fans dubbed the Flying Farmers began arriving in their own small planes to join the crowd.

Precise plowing requirements left no room for mistakes. Only the straightest and neatest furrows took prizes. Steady hands and keen eyes were vital for keeping every row 5-6 $1/2$ inches deep while cultivating an area nearly an acre in just two hours and fifteen minutes. One would assume that powerful horses and steel plows equaled lots of muscle and a men only event. Not necessarily so. Boys as young as nine showed their skill managing fistfuls of reins to take on those fields of red clover, and one year a woman not only took off her apron long enough to enter, but won. Now that's a woman who can hold her own - a plow and horses that is.

LEFT: Long retired wood beam walking plow at rest along the Riverwalk on Farm Families monument.

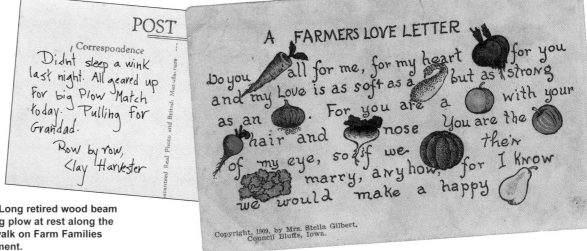

POST
Correspondence
Didn't sleep a wink last night. All geared up for big Plow Match today. Pulling for Grandad.

Row by row,
Clay Harvester

A FARMERS LOVE LETTER
Do you ___ all for me, for my heart ___ for you and my love is as soft as a ___ but as strong as an ___. For you are a ___ with your ___ hair and ___ nose You are the ___ of my eye, so if we ___ their ___ marry, anyhow, for I know we would make a happy ___

Copyright, 1909, by Mrs. Stella Gilbert, Council Bluffs, Iowa.

QUESTION: What does "being all in clover" mean?

M Make-a-Buck = Industry

On your mark, get set, grow! In the years before 1890, when Naperville was still a village, early industry was home-grown. The Stenger Brewery was built with stone from the Stenger quarry. Beers were brewed with grain from local farmers and chilled with ice from the local pond. The butter and cheese-making industry was produced with milk from the local cows. There was even an early industry for hand-rolled cigars.

When the railroad came to town in 1864, what began with a few quarry stones soon became a landslide. The late 1800s ushered in the founding of the first state and national banks, the opening of the Naperville Tile & Brick Works, the formation of the Naperville Fire Department, the arrival of the telephone and electric lighting for downtown streets. In 1890 the little village was incorporated as a city.

The early 1900s welcomed the arrival of indoor plumbing. The Naperville Lounge Co. became Kroehler Manufacturing Co. where "six for a quarter" Peter Kroehler sold six couches for $25. Washington Street and the business district saw the arrival of brick pavement along with the wireless telegraph. The Naperville Sun newspaper began publication in 1935 and Moser Lumber was born just in time for the post-World War II building boom.

There was no holding back now. From 19th century breweries and quarries to the 21st century high-tech corridor, Naperville was and still is a very attractive place to grow a business.

POST CARD

MESSAGE MAY BE WRITTEN ON THIS SIDE.   ADDRESS ONLY ON THIS SIDE.

Place the Stamp
ONE CENT
For United States
and Island Possessions,
Cuba, Canada and
Mexico.
TWO CENTS
For Foreign.

Dined and strolled in the old Kroehler Mfg. Co. If these walls could talk, what a tale they would tell. Great place to live, but bring your own furniture.

From 5th Avenue,
Ernest Cash

ABOVE: This once solid block of stone is 47" tall x 90" wide x 6" thick. Each letter is 10" high. It is on display in Naper Settlement's "Brushstrokes of the Past" history gallery.

BELOW: Sesquicentennial beer can, 1981.

Progress in Electronics

the First Factory that I workd in

Naperville Lounge Co., Naperville, Ill.

At one time the world's largest manufacturer of upholstered furniture with eight sites in the U.S. and two in Canada.

KROEHLER MFG. CO.

Today's 5th Avenue Station.

QUESTION: When the breweries ceased to brew beer, what food was successfully grown in the darkened buildings?

No Girls Allowed = YMCA

It all began in February 1909, after a successful series of tent revival meetings. While excitement was still high, a group of residents proposed the building of a YMCA as a gathering place for boys and men that would be an alternative to saloons and bars. This was a great idea, but once again there was no money. A plan was designed to raise the necessary funds by selling $5.00 advance memberships, called subscriptions, then using that money to construct a building that would include a gym and a swimming pool.

The plan worked! More than $26,000 was raised and the cornerstone was laid on Memorial Day, 1910. When funds began to run low, another $15,000 of advance memberships was raised in eight days! The "Y" was soon completed and was an instant success - for men and boys only. But ladies had also raised money by serving many formal dinners, so within six months of breaking ground, girls and women were admitted. The YMCA was on its way to becoming a welcoming community center serving the needs of all.

The "Y" proved to be much more than a gym and a swimming pool. During the war years, the Red Cross operated from the building. Over the years classes were offered in immigrant English, millinery and Russian conversation. From 1910 to the present, as the needs of the community changed, the YMCA changed along with it and is enjoyed today by thousands.

Cornerstone laying, 1910. Courtesy Naperville Sun.

Early Naperville "Y" gathering. Courtesy Heritage YMCA Group.

QUESTION: What do the letters YMCA stand for?

O Once upon a Town = Naper Settlement

NAPERVILLE, IL
DEC 16
-PM
1977
60540

PRE-EMPTION HOUSE

Pre-Emption House, 1834.
1931 photo courtesy Naperville Sun.

What you see IN THE BLACKSMITH SHOP

U.S. POSTAGE 3¢
CENTENNIAL OF BOOKER T. WASHINGTON

NAPER SETTLEMENT

This Space For Writing Messages

From a simple log house
to an opulent brick mansion,
this place has it all.
Wandered 13 acres with
my audio tour in hand.
Next stop - gift shop!
Earl E. Housman

EASTER SERIES NO.17

POST CARD

Place Stamp Here
Domestic One cent
Foreign Two cents

Log House, replica of 1843 original. The only building not native to Naperville, it was relocated from southern Illinois.

Volunteer lend a hand
USA 20c

Three cheers for volunteers! Without them there would be no Naper Settlement. This magical 19th century village, founded by volunteers in 1969 on the original site of the Martin Mitchell Mansion, is always in high gear thanks to its estimated 1,200 volunteers. No need for a time machine here. Just enter through the Pre-Emption House, Naperville's first hotel and tavern, and a 19th century world opens before you. Homes, from a Log House to a Victorian Mansion, print and blacksmith shops, a firehouse complete with the original Joe Naper hand pumper, a fort, a chapel, a one-room schoolhouse and a Conestoga wagon await your discovery.

Volunteers in authentic dress may be seen operating businesses and carrying on with everyday life - 19th century style. Special events include the annual Civil War Days in May and Christmas Memories in December. This living history village, comprised of thirty buildings, is nestled within the heart of 21st century Naperville. Don't miss it!

Martin Mitchell Mansion, 1883. Original to the site, it was first named Pine Craig.

QUESTION: Which President is said to have given a speech on a balcony of the Pre-Emption House?

P Pay the Toll = Old Plank Road

A toll way in Naperville in 1851? You bet! But hold your horses - and your pigs and cattle while you're at it. The earliest settlers needed a faster, safer way to take their grain and livestock into Chicago. Muddy trails were out, a wooden road was in.

Picture this: A toll road entirely handmade of three-inch thick oak planks, or boards, stretching from St. Charles to Chicago. No machines did the hard work for those pioneers. Every single twenty foot plank was sawed and carried by hand. Nails were too costly to use. They could only lay the wood side by side and cross their fingers.

If travelers paid a toll every five miles, man and beast could lumber along as far as they pleased. And if you think today's highways are crowded, you should have seen The Road. Imagine the clamor and smell as hundreds of loaded wagons and herds of farm animals plodded nose to tail. Speed did not exist. One side of the wooden road was for going to Chicago while the other side was for the return trip.

Stockholders made good money at first from all those tolls, but luck didn't last. Over years of heavy use and rugged weather the wood began to shift and warp and rot. In 1864, when the railroad entered the picture, the thousands of boards of Old Plank Road were torn up and given to the original investors. Not much of a consolation prize.

3¢

3¢

4¢

10¢

50¢

Plank Road toll rates for man and beast, 1851.

Plank Rd

POST CARD

THE CAMERA SHOP
Cedar Rapids, Ia.
306-2nd Avenue,

Took a free ride on my
bike on old Plank Road.
Tollbooths long gone.
Glad there are no splinters.

Rolling along,
Carrie Woods

PLACE
POSTAGE

UNITED STATES POSTAGE
1/2 CENTS 1/2

"Building the Plank Road" by Lester Schrader. Hand hewn planks laid one by one all the way to Chicago. Courtesy Naperville Heritage Society "Brushstrokes of the Past" history gallery.

"Beaubien Tavern" by Lester Schrader. A toll booth along the Plank Road. Courtesy Naperville Heritage Society "Brushstrokes of the Past" history gallery.

QUESTION: Today, a smoothly paved section of Plank Road still exists in Naperville. Do you know where it is?

Quill & Ink = Early Schools

22 USA — Public Education

Pulled the rope in the naper School bell tower. Needed both hands. Rang out loud and clear. First in line, Starr Lerner

HONORING THE TEACHERS OF AMERICA — NATIONAL EDUCATION ASSOCIATION 1857 1957 — UNITED STATES POSTAGE 3c

Naper report card, 1951.

GRADING SYSTEM

The Academy. Naperville, Ill.
Naper Academy, courtesy Naperville Heritage Society.
Dear Irene. This is where you and I will go this fall. Sincerely, Frank.

Academy class photo, Courtesy Naper School.

With lessons over, We're in Clover, Run and Shout, School is out
WINNER SCHOOL CONTEST 1917
COPYRIGHT, 1916 T. C. WILLSON

The road to World Class status began in 1832 in a one-room log schoolhouse, thanks to none other than Captain Naper just one year after he arrived. It seems education for their children was as important to parents in the 1800s as it is today. In 1850 Captain Naper donated land and stone from his quarry to begin the construction of Naper Academy. It took three years to build the three-story school because they kept running out of lumber and money. The job did get done, one floor at a time, and the West Side Academy, as it was first called, opened as a private school in December of 1852.

Students aged eight to twenty from as far away as Wisconsin attended, sometimes sleeping in the classrooms and providing their own candles for light. In 1859 the Academy became a public school. All pupils were welcome and some classes soared to over seventy students per room. Students took turns standing in the aisles.

The town was growing fast and that meant more and more children to educate. In 1928 Naper Academy was demolished and the current Naper School was built. By then that wasn't the only game in town. Less than a mile away, Ellsworth School, known then as "the little east side school," was up and thriving. Naper Academy's original bell tower still tops Naper School and rings daily calling students to classes. Naperville is now a community with two large school districts and dozens of public and parochial schools. That little log schoolhouse was but a baby step on the path to the nationally acclaimed education Naperville enjoys today.

QUESTION: School was closed for major events three times before 1875. What were they?

R Roads Gallery = Founding Fathers

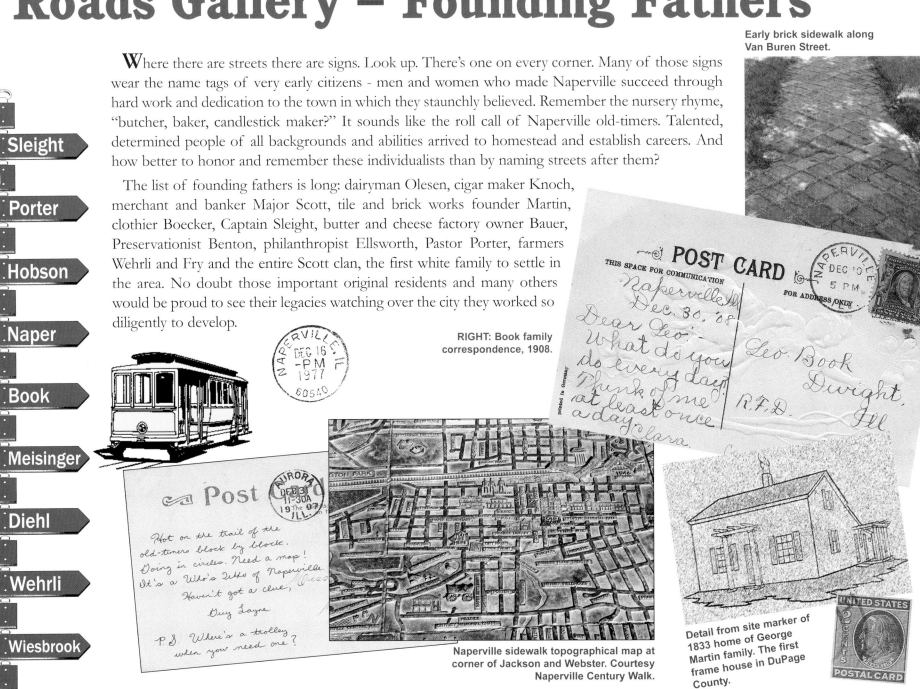

Benton · **Sleight** · **Ellsworth** · **Porter** · **Olesen** · **Hobson** · **Gartner** · **Naper** · **Martin** · **Book** · **Modaff** · **Meisinger** · **Bauer** · **Diehl** · **Rickert** · **Wehrli** · **Royce** · **Wiesbrook** · **Drendel**

Where there are streets there are signs. Look up. There's one on every corner. Many of those signs wear the name tags of very early citizens - men and women who made Naperville succeed through hard work and dedication to the town in which they staunchly believed. Remember the nursery rhyme, "butcher, baker, candlestick maker?" It sounds like the roll call of Naperville old-timers. Talented, determined people of all backgrounds and abilities arrived to homestead and establish careers. And how better to honor and remember these individualists than by naming streets after them?

The list of founding fathers is long: dairyman Olesen, cigar maker Knoch, merchant and banker Major Scott, tile and brick works founder Martin, clothier Boecker, Captain Sleight, butter and cheese factory owner Bauer, Preservationist Benton, philanthropist Ellsworth, Pastor Porter, farmers Wehrli and Fry and the entire Scott clan, the first white family to settle in the area. No doubt those important original residents and many others would be proud to see their legacies watching over the city they worked so diligently to develop.

Early brick sidewalk along Van Buren Street.

RIGHT: Book family correspondence, 1908.

POST CARD

Naperville Ill. Dec. 30, '08. Dear Leo:- What do you do every day? Think of me at least once a day. Clara.

Leo. Book Dwight, R.F.D. Ill

Post

Hot on the trail of the old-timers block by block. Doing in circles. Need a map! It's a Who's Who of Naperville. Haven't got a clue,

Guy Layne

P.S. Where's a trolley when you need one?

Naperville sidewalk topographical map at corner of Jackson and Webster. Courtesy Naperville Century Walk.

Detail from site marker of 1833 home of George Martin family. The first frame house in DuPage County.

QUESTION: Two main downtown streets are named for famous men in early American history who did **NOT** reside in Naperville. Who were they?

Stake Your Claim = Joe Naper & Friends

Something may TURNIP YET

UNITED STATES POSTAGE 3¢ — THIS IS THE PLACE — 1847 THE UTAH CENTENNIAL 1947

4¢ U.S. POSTAGE — THE HOMESTEAD ACT 1862 1962

U.S. 5¢ HOMEMAKERS

3¢ SOO LOCKS-1855 SAULT SAINTE MARIE 1955 U.S. POSTAGE — A CENTURY OF GREAT LAKES TRANSPORTATION

The old and the new. Joseph and Almeda headstones together in Naperville Cemetery.

WIFE ALMEDA LANDON DIED FEB. 6, 1855 AGE 85 YEARS — HUSBAND CAPT. JOSEPH DIED AUG. 17, 1862 AGE 64 YEARS — FOUNDERS OF NAPER NAPERVILLE

POST CARD.
THE ADDRESS ONLY TO BE WRITTEN

PUTTING DOWN ROOTS.
X MARKS THE SPOT.
WISH US LUCK,
GRANT LANDERS

CENTENARY OF THE TELEGRAPH 3¢ — WHAT HATH GOD WROUGHT 1844 1944 — UNITED STATES POSTAGE

"Spirit of 1831" by Lester Schrader. Courtesy Naperville Heritage Society "Brushstrokes of the Past" history gallery.

Due to the scarcity of paper, precious postcards were put to use more than once. In this case they were used as patterns for quilt pieces.

How did pioneer adventurers choose the best places to make their dreams come true? With great care, as the strong and courageous Naper brothers, Captain Joseph and John, would tell you.

After sailing from Ohio through Lakes Erie, Huron and Michigan to Chicago's Fort Dearborn in 1831, they headed west by schooner wagon to settle along the DuPage River. When they discovered wildlife for hunting, trees for lumber, fertile land for farming, rivers for water and the friendly Scott and Hobson clans already established as neighbors, the brothers plunged into a frontier life far more challenging than they had ever imagined. Remarkably, they made a go of it that first year in spite of brutal weather, devastating illness, acute loneliness and a diet of buckwheat cakes and turnips, two crops that could be grown and harvested before winter set in.

Known for their leadership and determination, the Napers wasted no time making those dreams come true. Within months a log school house was erected, a sawmill and store were underway and a dam was built. Within a few years the tiny population exploded, building mushroomed, local government was in place, and the rest, as they say, is history. And how!

QUESTION: What did it mean in the 1800s to "stake a claim?" Why was it crucial to do so?

Here Comes   Captain Joe Naper March   And the Band Played On   Naperville Municipal Band March   Strike Up Another Show

Keller

Toot Your Horn = Municipal Band

Municipal Band circa 1940s.
Courtesy Naperville Sun.

UNITED STATES POSTAGE
2¢ JOHN PHILIP SOUSA

POST CARD

THIS SIDE FOR CORRESPONDENCE

THE ADDRESS
ON

All tuned up,
Hope for clear skies.
Ready for encores.
Let the music begin.
Melody March

34

Nothing fancy - come as you are.

"Naperville's Own" bas relief courtesy Naperville
Century Walk.

If you want to hear an ear-splitting cannon boom or celebrate Christmas in July, then grab a blanket and march over to a performance of the award-winning Naperville Municipal Band. Since 1859 it has played by various names: Naperville Brass Band, Light Guard Band, Kroehler Lounge Factory Band and Naperville City Band. In 1929 it became the Naperville Municipal Band. It was men only until 1933 when its constitution was amended to admit women - and it has never looked or sounded better.

In 1889 a bandstand was built in Central Park for the Light Guard Band. A replica can be seen today at Naper Settlement. In 1966 the second bandstand was replaced with a permanent band shell. But the best was yet to come. 2003 saw the dedication of a bigger and bolder band shell on the site of the new Community Concert Center. From June through August, Thursday evenings in Naperville are alive with music. And it's all free! Come early, you won't want to miss a beat of this toe-tapping experience.

QUESTION: In 1940 what unique project did the band undertake to raise money for new uniforms?

Central Park Civil
War cannon

Under the Weather = Sanatorium

Courtesy Naperville Heritage Society.

Sleeping Tents Edwards Sanitarium. Naperville, Ill.   A.B.H.

POST CARD

Sniffles, sneezes, coughs, achoos
Papercuts, bruises,
tummyache blues
Scrapes and rashes, measles and
mumps
Mysterious ailments and
assorted bumps

To your health,
E.R. Ward

1917

Edward Sanatorium, Naperville, Ill.—4319-R

Courtesy Naperville Heritage Society, 1915.

Emily Bissell
Crusader Against Tuberculosis
USA 15c

giving
BLOOD
saves lives   6

UNITED STATES POSTAGE
FOUNDER OF THE
CLARA BARTON
AMERICAN RED CROSS   3¢

Letters
Lift Spirits
USA 15c

What was one of the most feared diseases of the 20th century? It went by the names of TB, tuberculosis or consumption, and caused difficulty breathing and severe coughing. If left untreated, it would result in death. If diagnosed early, it could be cured with many weeks of rest, fresh air and exercise. It was commonly thought that "the cure" had to be taken in a warm climate, but in 1907, Naperville pioneered the local treatment of TB when it opened Edward Sanatorium.

What began with fourteen beds soon grew to one hundred. It was so successful that companies named Sears, Wards and Swift paid for the construction of open-air cottages for their tubercular employees. Patients rested and slept in outdoor "shacks" so that they could be constantly surrounded by fresh air. By 1920 the wooden sanatorium burned to the ground. It was immediately rebuilt as a fire-proof structure in 1921. Hundreds of lives were saved thanks to the dedication of "The San."

After World War II new medications were discovered to treat tuberculosis and fewer patients needed to be isolated. In 1956 Edward Sanatorium became Edward Hospital and the saving of lives continues to this day.

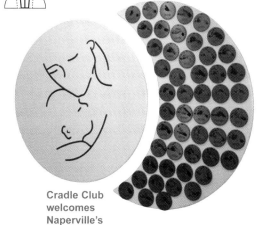

Cradle Club welcomes Naperville's newest.

Four hundred beds strong, Edward Hospital, 2004.

The Ins and Outs of Edward Hospital.

N S X

QUESTION: Where does the name "Edward" in Edward Hospital come from?

V Voices of the Past = Genevieve Towsley

Ever try counting on your fingers? If you tried counting everything a young lady named Genevieve did, you'd run out of hands before you'd barely started. From her childhood in Idaho's Snake River Valley to her long life as a devoted friend to Naperville, that ambitious little girl never stopped. From camping, ranching, piano playing, tending sheep, teaching Sunday School, gardening, raising poultry and saving Buffalo nickels to buy her first horse, you name it and Genevieve (Brayton) Towsley did it well and with a passion. And always, always reading and writing.

How she enjoyed words and the memories they could capture! For twenty-two years she hand wrote a column called Sky-Lines for a local newspaper, both preserving the past and promoting the present of her beloved Naperville, the town she called "family." She wouldn't recognize her cherished city today with its Carillon Tower, Municipal Center, Riverwalk, sky-high condos, multi-million dollar businesses and countless opportunities for citizens of every age and ethnicity.

Read around the border for the table of contents.

Mrs. Towsley, 1907-1995, at work on Sky-Lines. Courtesy Naperville Sun.

THE AMERICAN WOMAN

"OUR REPUBLIC AND ITS PRESS WILL RISE OR FALL TOGETHER"

Ran onto Genevieve in town. Sat down beside her and whispered in her ear, "Thanks for the memories."

Typing away,
Page Scribner

"Genevieve" courtesy Naperville Century Walk

If Naperville ever had a godmother, Mrs. Towsley was the one. Little did she imagine that someday her likeness would be permanently seated at one of the busiest intersections in the town she loved so much. It's a most appropriate spot because she was one of the busiest and most productive fans of the little town that could.

QUESTION: Where did Mrs. Towsley attend college?

Voices of the Past = Lester Schrader

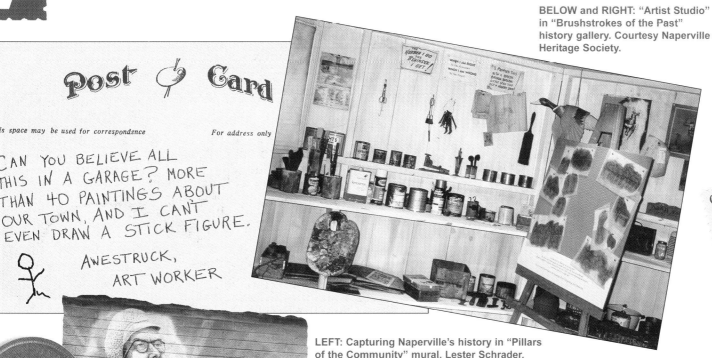

Post Card

This space may be used for correspondence   *For address only*

CAN YOU BELIEVE ALL
THIS IN A GARAGE? MORE
THAN 40 PAINTINGS ABOUT
OUR TOWN, AND I CAN'T
EVEN DRAW A STICK FIGURE.

AWESTRUCK,
ART WORKER

BELOW and RIGHT: "Artist Studio" in "Brushstrokes of the Past" history gallery. Courtesy Naperville Heritage Society.

Grandma Moses

6c U.S. Postage

USA 13c

LEFT: Capturing Naperville's history in "Pillars of the Community" mural. Lester Schrader, 1907-1984. Courtesy Naperville Century Walk.

What is your very favorite thing to do? If you had had the privilege of posing that question to a certain young boy who moved to Naperville in 1908, his answer would have been easy. More than anything else, Lester E. Schrader loved to draw and paint, and throughout his long life, that never changed.

As a child he drew horses and Native Americans. As a man he did the same, painting in remarkable detail picture after picture of the saga of Naperville's earliest days. Naperville was in his blood.

Lester never practiced and had only one art lesson in his life. From his first painting at age three on the underside of his mother's ironing board, to the final painting in his fascinating Naperville series, his folk art style invites the "reader" of his pictures to enter into days of old. Even though he always worked alone in his garage, his pictures are populated with more people than you can count. When you look at his paintings, be sure to look for Les, as he often painted himself right into the action.

If Mrs. Towsley's collected news columns are remembered as the Naperville bible, certainly Mr. Schrader's works of art are the stained glass windows of the town. Each is the result of months and sometimes years of intense local research. Every canvas is a painted snapshot of the past. Naperville's heritage is Les's gift to the community where his talent didn't go unnoticed.

QUESTION: Painting over forty pictures of historic Naperville was Lester Schrader's hobby. What was his regular job?

W When Johnny Comes Marching Home
= PATRIOTS

HONORING
U.S. SERVICEMEN

PRISONERS
OF WAR

MISSING AND
KILLED IN ACTION

UNITED 6¢ STATES

AMERICA
ON
GUARD

$5.

U.S. POSTAL
SAVINGS

1941

Post Card

THIS SPACE MAY BE USED FOR
CORRESPONDENCE

From the Black Hawk War
to the War on Terrorism,
this town remembers its
heroes. Naperville is
proud of its own.

Respectfully yours,

Victor Service, G. I.

"Unfurl
our Flag before us;
Fling wide our banner fair;
Let the Stars and Stripes
float o'er us,
And gaily kiss the air."

Honoring
Those Who Served

USA
29

Desert Shield ★ Desert Storm

These IMMORTAL CHAPLAINS...
INTERFAITH IN ACTION

3¢ UNITED STATES POSTAGE 3¢

THE NATIONAL GUARD OF THE U.S.
IN WAR
IN PEACE

THE OLDEST MILITARY ORGANIZATION IN THE US

Vietnam Veterans Memorial USA 20c

ABOVE: War on Terrorism memorial and segments from "Wall of Faces." Naperville Municipal Center.

VETERAN
1812
1814

WII
WAR

QUESTION: Has anyone in your
family served in the military
during wartime?

Cemetery medallions commemorating wartime service.

GAR
1861
1865

WORLD WAR
US
1917-1918

OFFICERS and SOLDIERS

AMERICA on GUARD

USA 22

WOMEN IN OUR ARMED SERVICES
UNITED STATES 3¢ OF AMERICA

UNITED STATES POSTAGE 3 CENTS
1790 U.S. COAST GUARD 1945

3¢ UNITED STATES POSTAGE U.S. NAVY

WIN THE WAR
3¢ UNITED STATES POSTAGE 3¢

THIS SIDE FOR CORRESPONDENCE.

POST CARD

One look at the memorials shows that Napervillians have served in every conflict since the Black Hawk War.

"While above them floats 'Old Glory', Boon to all the world oppressed."

1861-1865

ABOVE: World War I Doughboy, Burlington Square Park.

BELOW: Civil War memorial, Naperville Cemetery.

IN MEMORY OF THE SOLDIERS OF THE CIVIL WAR 1861-1865

G.A.R.

3¢ UNITED STATES POSTAGE HONORING THOSE WHO HAVE SERVED 3¢

X Xtra! Xtra! = Hot News

Huffman Street flood, mid-1950s.

Which of the following actually happened in Naperville?

A. Fire destroyed the largest church in town and fire engines were unable to help.

B. Train wreck killed 47 and injured more than 100.

C. Twenty-two inches of rain fell causing the worst flood in 100 years.

D. Full grown pigs took a ride on one of nature's quirks called a freshet.

E. A Dorothy kind of cyclone blew away a 125-foot section of a brick building.

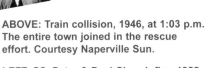

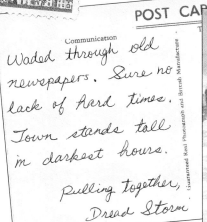

Waded through old newspapers. Sure no lack of hard times. Town stands tall in darkest hours.

Pulling together,
Dread Storm

ABOVE: Train collision, 1946, at 1:03 p.m. The entire town joined in the rescue effort. Courtesy Naperville Sun.

LEFT: SS. Peter & Paul Church fire, 1922. Courtesy Naperville Heritage Society.

BELOW: Nearly every area farmer reported a loss from the midnight storm of 1913 that devastated the Kroehler Lounge Factory.

"1857 Flood" by Lester Schrader. The freshet packed huge cakes of ice against the stone bridge. Water swept over the banks on both sides, wiping out homes and businesses. Courtesy Naperville Heritage Society.

Sadly, all of the above troubles and more are a part of Naperville's past. Skies have not always been sunny and winds have not always been calm. The town has certainly had its share of major disasters but always with unexpected and positive results. It would take more than floods and fires, clashes and crashes to subdue the spirit of that little dot on the Illinois map that stands for unity and harmony. In times of serious threat, her citizens never fail to rally to the rescue of the place they hold so dear.

QUESTION: How was the expression, "Xtra! Xtra!" used in the newspaper business?

Y Yours Truly = Postal Service

Dear Naperville,

Congratulations on a tough job well done. How in the world did you do it? I hear you have not one but two post offices with mail trucks and mail carriers delivering door to door six days a week. But I'm sure that's an exaggeration. Why, in my day it took months for a single letter to reach us on the prairie, and often the mail never made it at all. Before we had a post office the mail arrived by horse, wagon and bugle. That's right, when you heard the bugle blast you hurried on over to Howard Hall with your fingers crossed. How our womenfolk longed for news from back home. I saw more than one lady sit right down and weep with joy to have word of her kinfolk after endless waiting. I guess just about everybody loves a letter.

It wasn't long before our little town became a stagecoach stop between Chicago and Galena. Mail was dropped off at PawPaw, our first post office. Three address changes later an official post office cornerstone was laid at the corner of Washington and Benton streets. Word has it that landmark is still there. Stop by and see for yourself.

Pen in hand,

Joseph P. Naper

Local postman Julian Ory with 1928 mail truck.

QUESTION: In 1906 what was the heaviest mail delivery day?

It's not a bird, it's not a plane...

Winter snow means more dough.

Those zany names!

What? No drawers?

Sprechen sie Deutsch?

Z Zany = Believe It or Not!

Travel on Old Plank Road was free on Sundays for anyone going to church.

In the late 1800s many Naperville classes were taught only in German.

In 1929 the dirigible Graf Zeppelin passed over Naperville for five minutes headed toward Chicago on its world-encircling flight.

The Haases, a Naperville family, had nine sons who formed their own baseball team. And play they did. Four went on to play professionally.

Naperville almost had a shorter name. Many residents were unhappy with the addition of "ville" to the founder's name and wanted the simpler name of "Naper" instead.

As with many frontier towns in the 1800s, saloons were popular spots for men to sip and sit with friends. In 1875 a law closed those hangouts whenever the town fire bell sounded to announce an emergency.

Postkarte

An

Love the wild side of the Good old Days. This is my kind of town.

Too Cool,
Marvel Ripley

BELOW: Graf Zeppelin at home in Germany.

Luftschiff „Graf Zeppelin" (L. Z. 127) wird aus der Halle gezogen.

(Strasse u. Haush...)

NAPERVILLE, ILL
DEC 31
2 PM
1907

Certain areas of Naperville had an international ring to their names. The Naper Settlement visitor path is located in a part of Naperville that was known as "Canada." Another area of town was known as Copenhagen Corners and still other neighborhoods were nick-named Quality Hill, Stump Town, Piety Hill, Park Addition and Goose Pimple Heights.

Those Kroehler employees really earned their wages. Carrying heavy couches on their backs was hard work, especially when they had to walk as far as four blocks to waiting boxcars under the weight of that furniture. The leather on the backs of their special jackets had to be replaced twice a month. Now that's called a hard day's work.

Pennsylvania Dutch settler boys didn't have many wardrobe worries. They wore no overshoes, overcoats or underwear!

Monthly Horse Market Days attracted gypsies caravanning in covered wagons.

Although today it looks like one very large complex under one roof, the old Kroehler Furniture Factory was a combination of no less than seventeen separate, smaller buildings. Isn't that hard to picture?

Winter schoolteachers earned more than summer staff because they had to tote wood and stoke stoves to warm the classrooms.

QUESTION: **What do you think is Zany in Naperville today?**

? = **Answers**

A $500

B   Naperville All-Stars

C   Approximately 360,000 books

D   Surprise! It was not from a local quarry. They were imported from France.

E   As of printing the number is 136,400

F   6.2 million gallons of water

G   The "hand," a measure of four inches

H   St. Patrick's Day, Memorial Day and Last Fling Labor Day

I   (adj.) 1. unequalled, matchless, peerless   2. tops, the best, awesome

J   Living conditions were terribly cramped, food was scarce and the noise was ceaseless.

K   Chicago Fire soccer team

L   Being all in clover means being wealthy or well-to-do. In this instance wealth was not measured in money but rather in hands-on community pride and plowing progress.

M   Mushrooms. Naperville was a major supplier to both Campbell's and Jewel Foods.

N   Young Men's Christian Association

O   Abraham Lincoln, Joe Naper's friend from state government

P   Plank Road runs east-west from the viaduct at Columbia to Ogden Avenue. Wind along this paved road and you will follow in the footsteps of those who made Naperville history.

Q   Naper first closed in 1865 when Robert E. Lee surrendered to Ulysses S. Grant, thus ending the Civil War. It closed for three months in 1866 due to a small pox epidemic. It closed a third time in 1870 for Cornerstone Day at North Central College.

R   George Washington and Thomas Jefferson

S   To stake a claim meant to mark and legally register the boundaries of a plot of land in your name so that no one else could claim it as his own.

T   They made a color movie titled, "You're in the Movies." It was a silent film accompanied by live narration that was shown in Pfeiffer Hall at North Central College.

U   Mrs. Eldora Spalding founded it as a memorial to her first husband, Edward Gaylord.

V   She attended North Central College in Naperville where she earned high honors.

V   He was a sign painter.

W   The adults in your family can help you with this.

X   It was shouted by street corner newsboys hawking special edition papers of the hottest breaking stories.

Y   Valentine's Day

Z   Have fun with this one!

Spillover = Couldn't Quite Fit

A = Taxi service to the Naperville depot was horse-drawn only until 1923, when the first motorized taxi service began.

B = A basketball team from Ellsworth School high school was first to use the name Exiles in 1910, when the principal refused to allow the formation of a school team. In 1913 the name was adopted by a baseball team.

C = A second show of community spirit occurred in 1934 when patrons held a "book shower" to replenish the library shelves.

D = From the Pennsylvania Dutch came Shoo-fly pie. This sweet concoction of molasses and brown sugar gave diners cause to "shoo" away flies.

E = A Naperville hot spot in the Roaring 20s, the Spanish Tea Room sported a fountain and a fish pond and attracted restaurateurs from Chicago. A complete chicken dinner could be had for 60 cents.

F = From 1933 to 1942 the CCC had 92 camps in IL, two of which were in Naperville. Camp McDowell saw 3,800 men pass through its army-style barracks during its four years of operation. Bridges across the DuPage River, picnic shelters, a boathouse and bridle paths were constructed. Trees were planted in Pioneer and Burlington Parks. Illinois had 60 million trees planted, with an estimated three billion trees planted nationwide, all by the CCC.

G = A stampede of full-size carousel horses, hand-decorated by local artists, took the town by storm the summer of 2002. Keep a sharp eye and you may see one stabled in a yard or business.

H = Both the 1917 Home Coming and the 1931 Centennial booklets are alive and well at Nichols Library. If you are looking for homecoming queen Jane Latshaw today, you can find her likeness at the entrance to the Riverwalk. Always a queen to her Billy.

I = The first Arbor Day was celebrated in Nebraska in 1872 thanks to Julius Sterling Morton who served as President Cleveland's Secretary of Agriculture. Morton's son, Joy, later founded the Morton Arboretum. President Nixon created a National Arbor Day in 1970. Today all 50 states and many countries celebrate Arbor Day. So on the last Friday in April, plant a tree and give it a hug.

J = (cont'd from border) ". . . There are only two small rooms and six families to occupy them. . . There are twenty-two children. . . And here I am in a crazy chamber in the midst of this confusion, sitting on my feet, with my paper on a chair, scribbling to you. We stayed at Chicago nearly four weeks. . . Two months ago we were quietly pursuing our labors, thought not of danger or interruption. . . But what a contrast! Tell F. I thank her for her letter. I will answer it in a year or two if I have an opportunity to send it. I must bid you good-bye. Write again, and do not forget your sincere friend and sister."
Caroline Strong

1896
James Nichols
Author/Publisher

K = A tradition of the past, state Booster Clubs began around 1912. The purpose was to recruit students to the college through floats, parades and prizes.

Too Good to Omit

Fire Pumper
1860s
USA 20¢

1935
Harold Moser
Founder - Naperville Sun

GENERALS COMMANDING U. S. ARMY.

George Washington.	9 years.
Henry Knox.	1 "
Josiah Harmer.	3 "
Arthur St. Clair.	5 "
James Wilkinson.	14 "
Henry Dearborn.	3 "
Jacob Brown.	13 "
Alex. McComb.	13 "
Winfield Scott.	20 "
Geo. B. McClellan.	1 "
Henry W. Halleck.	2 "
U. S. Grant.	5 "
W. T. Sherman.	14 "
Philip Sheridan.	5 "
J. M. Schofield.	7 "
Nelson B. Miles.	—

L = Talent of all sorts was on display. Prizes were coveted for everything from leaf yeast bread, hand-knit mittens, stitched razzle-dazzles, paper flower collections, frosted creams, squash pie, hen and chicks tufted rugs, late potatoes and even pupil compositions.

M = Adolf Coors got his start at Stenger Brewery but left for Colorado rather than marry a Stenger daughter. Hence, Coors beer in CO.

N = Did you spot the bowling pin on the page? The first YMCA on Washington had a bowling alley in the basement!

O = Don't want someone else to grab the land you want? Better register a claim at the Pre-Emption House before heading back to collect your family and possessions.

P = It cost $2,000 per mile to build Old Plank Road.

Q = Hobson School, one of the oldest one-room schools in the county, was built for under $100 and opened its doors in 1843.

R = Harold Moser (1914-2001) For 50 years Naperville's unsung benefactor and builder. A gentleman as well as a gentle man.

S = Five families joined the Napers' voyage from Ohio aboard the "Telegraph." Can you find it in the painting?

T = The Civil War cannon in Central Park no longer fires. When a cannon blast is needed on the 4th of July, one is trucked in from the Civil War re-enactors.

U = Sleeping quarters were open-air shacks. The Naperville Band and North Central College would regularly present entertainment for recovering patients.

V = Genevieve never hesitated to speak out when she saw injustice and won many awards for doing so. She helped launch Little Friends, Inc., a private, non-profit organization serving special needs children and adults.

V = Les painted so precisely that he used a brush with a single bristle to paint eyeglasses. Extra credit if you can find his trusty pipes, his original paint palette, an old stapler and a horse or two in his workshop.

W = Soldiers from Naperville who enlisted to fight in the Civil War began their tour of duty by marching to Wheaton to catch the train heading south. "When Johnny Comes Marching Home" is a Civil War era song written for the Army and Navy.

X = The threat of fire was a constant worry in early years. Prior to 1874 Naperville had no fire equipment and looked to Aurora for assistance. In 1874 for $1,000, the town brought a hand pumper nicknamed "Joe Naper" to town. You can see it displayed today at Naper Settlement.

Y = Paw Paw Station, named for the paw paw trees nearby, was Naperville's first post office and a stop on the stage coach line.

Z = Zany - 1. whimsically comical 2. out of the ordinary 3. an oddity

P.S. Play It Safe = Safety Town

Ruff and ready!

Courtesy Naperville Sun

Ever watchful for Naperville's kids.

Gone are the days
of the one sheriff town.
By foot, by bike or car,
wherever you are,
a badge is waiting
to help you.

Keeping out of trouble,
Chase Justice

A pint-sized town within a town at the corner of River Road and Aurora Avenue.

Has anyone ever told you that you just can't be too careful? What that means is no matter where you are or what you are doing, safety is #1. Being a city that thrives on children and families, Naperville offers enough unique and exciting opportunities to learn about safety to last a lifetime. All the better for living straight.

Youngsters can enjoy days or weeks of safety sessions at Naperville's own city within a city. Years ago the Junior Women's Club liked what was happening to safety all across the USA. In 1977 they joined the Safety Town movement and used little collapsible, cardboard, buildings set up in school gymnasiums to teach boys and girls just what safety was all about. By 1996 enough Naperville citizens and businesses knew a great thing when they saw it, and raised funds to build an entire town - Safety Town.

Its own realistic world of permanent kid-sized buildings, mini streets, a train on a track and a cool classroom for warm summer days, the Town now provides a place and space for hundreds of Naperville's youngest to learn personal safety for home and away. Who better than local police and fire department experts to demonstrate all there is to know about playing it safe in all the right places? Safety Town and Naperville: double the safety, double the fun.

TWO OF AMERICA'S FINEST LAW ENFORCEMENT OFFICERS

With best regards from cartoonist Dick Locher.

Naperville's one and only Officer Friendly, a.k.a. Mayor Pradel, in fine company with Dick Tracy.

Naperville

Sources

"Arbor Day." TreeHelp.com. 28 October 2003 <http://www.arbor-day.net/>.

Cowlishaw, Mary Lou. *This Band's Been Here Quite A Spell . . . 1859-1981*. The Naperville Municipal Band, Inc., 1981.

Frolick, Sharon and Richard L. Ruehrwein. *Naper Settlement: A 19th Century Village*. Lawrenceburg, IN: The Creative Company, 1999.

Fry, John. *"My Dad Says . . ."* Naperville, IL: Wheatland View Publishing, Inc., 2000.

Lebeau, Pierre and Ann Durkin Keating. *North Central College and Naperville: A Shared History*. Naperville, IL: North Central College, 1995.

"Mission and History." The Morton Arboretum. Morton Arboretum. 30 October 2003 <http://www.mortonarb.org/>.

Naperville Area Farm Families History. Naperville Farmers' Riverwalk Committee. Bloom Printing Corp., 1983.

Naperville Centennial 1831-1931. Fort Payne Chapter Daughters of the American Revolution. Naperville, IL, 1975.

"Roosevelt's Tree Army: A Brief History of the Civilian Conservation Corps." Civilian Conservation Corps. 28 October 2003 <http://www.cccalumni.org/history1.html>.

Schmus, Jean. "The Centennial Beach Story." *Naperville Sun*, 19 June 1952.

Schrader, Lester. *Landmarks In Naperville 1831-1981*.

Souvenir of the Naperville Home Coming. Hammersmith Kortmeyer Co., 1917.

"States Boost North Central College: A Look at Booster Clubs." North Central College Archives. North Central College. 30 October 2003 <http://www.noctrl.edu/library_ncc/archives/exhibits/Summer03/intro.html>.

Towsley, Genevieve. *A View of Historic Naperville*. Sproul, Peg ed. 3rd printing. Naperville, IL: Naperville Sun, 1979.

YMCA in America, 1851-2001: A History of Accomplishment Over 150 Years. Maier, Daniel ed. 2000.

The end.

In the palmy days of Burlington Park.18 –1901

ON THE BANKS OF THE DUPAGE RIVER, NAPERVILLE, ILL.

And so amid Life's duties,
I sometimes pause, and let
Fond Memory lead me backward,
With a faint sigh of regret,
To the many scenes of pleasure,
And the joys I'll ne'er forget. H.D.A. 1904.